STEAM GUIDES IN TRANSPORTATION

Ruth M. Kirk

Rourke
Educational Media

rourkeeducationalmedia.com

Before Reading:

Building Academic Vocabulary and Background Knowledge

Before reading a book, it is important to tap into what your child or students already know about the topic. This will help them develop their vocabulary, increase their reading comprehension, and make connections across the curriculum.

1. *Look at the cover of the book. What will this book be about?*
2. *What do you already know about the topic?*
3. *Let's study the Table of Contents. What will you learn about in the book's chapters?*
4. *What would you like to learn about this topic? Do you think you might learn about it from this book? Why or why not?*
5. *Use a reading journal to write about your knowledge of this topic. Record what you already know about the topic and what you hope to learn about the topic.*
6. *Read the book.*
7. *In your reading journal, record what you learned about the topic and your response to the book.*
8. *After reading the book complete the activities below.*

Content Area Vocabulary
Read the list. What do these words mean?

altitude
component
congested
corrode
efficiency
entrepreneur
friction
habitable
humanitarian
insulate
repel
urban

After Reading:

Comprehension and Extension Activity

After reading the book, work on the following questions with your child or students in order to check their level of reading comprehension and content mastery.

1. *Name some of the advances being discovered in transportation.* (Summarize)
2. *What is one benefit of not using a car?* (Inferring)
3. *How does an e-bike work?* (Asking questions)
4. *What are some ways drones are being used?* (Text to self connection)
5. *What does STEAM stand for?* (Asking questions)

Extension Activity

Transportation gets us from one place to another. But, there are drawbacks, such as pollution and lack of space to enjoy habitable areas, like parks and recreational facilities. Think of ways you could reduce relying on cars, buses, and other forms of transportation that cause these problems. In a notebook or journal, write down alternative ways you and your family could get from place to place. Share your ideas with them and see if they can help!

TABLE OF CONTENTS

MOVING IDEAS

Transportation is about more than how you get to school. It's about how the clothes you're wearing crossed the ocean. And how the satellite that transmits your favorite television show made it into orbit. And even how your running shoes can still bounce after your tenth 5K race.

Today's transportation relies on ideas and innovations from science, technology, engineering, art, and math, or STEAM for short. Let's zoom in on some of those ideas. They're approaching at rocket speed!

Hyperloop: Will Hype Become Reality?

The world may be about to get a whole new form of transportation called the Hyperloop. It would travel at more than 700 miles (1,127 kilometers) per hour and use solar power. Tubes would be mounted above ground, on pylons, or supports. A capsule-shaped pod would zip through the tubes like an air hockey puck. The Hyperloop system could also be built below ground or underwater. It could carry passengers or cargo.

Friction and air resistance are two forces that can slow down any vehicle. The Hyperloop pods would avoid friction with the tubes by floating on an extremely thin layer of air. To lower air resistance, machines on the outside of the pods would transfer air from in front of the pods to behind them.

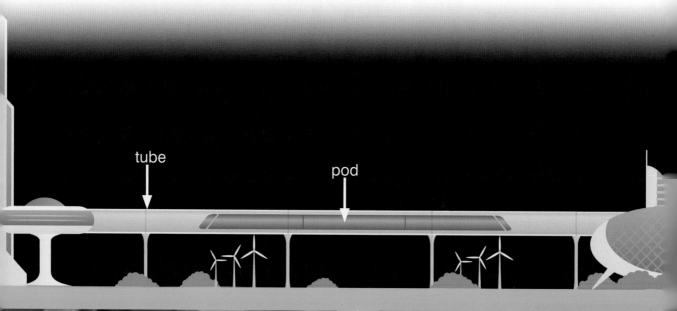

tube

pod

STEAM
Fast Fact!

Engineers working on the Hyperloop want to eliminate as much friction and air resistance from the system as possible. Look at these pictures. Which ones are opposites, and how do they relate to speed?

Since California is a likely location for the Hyperloop, people are concerned about what would happen to it in an earthquake. California sits on top of a fault line where two slabs of the Earth's crust meet. When stress causes the slabs to slip, earthquakes take place. Engineers would need to design the Hyperloop pylons to withstand violent shaking.

California's San Andreas fault, site of the 1906 earthquake in San Franciso, is about 800 miles (1,287 kilometers) long, running west of San Francisco and east of Los Angeles.

San Andreas fault ⟶

STEAM Profile !

Elon Musk, a transportation **entrepreneur**, first proposed the idea of the Hyperloop in 2013. He said it would be both faster and cheaper than the high-speed train the state of California was planning.

Using an approach called crowdsourcing, Musk invited anyone to contribute ideas and expertise to make the Hyperloop a reality. Respected engineers and business leaders have done just that. Different companies working on the Hyperloop have their own variations of the basic concept.

Elon Musk

A group of architecture students from the University of California at Los Angeles have focused on the artistic and human aspects of the Hyperloop. They realized that traveling in a pod with no windows at a high speed could be scary.

To help passengers relax, the students designed artistic scenes including forests and starry skies that would be projected onto the walls of the pods. The students also built models of possible Hyperloop station designs, ranging from tall and grand to low and circular.

STEAM in Action!

Making the Hyperloop a reality will rely on every aspect of STEAM! Can you list some ways each STEAM field might contribute to a project like this?

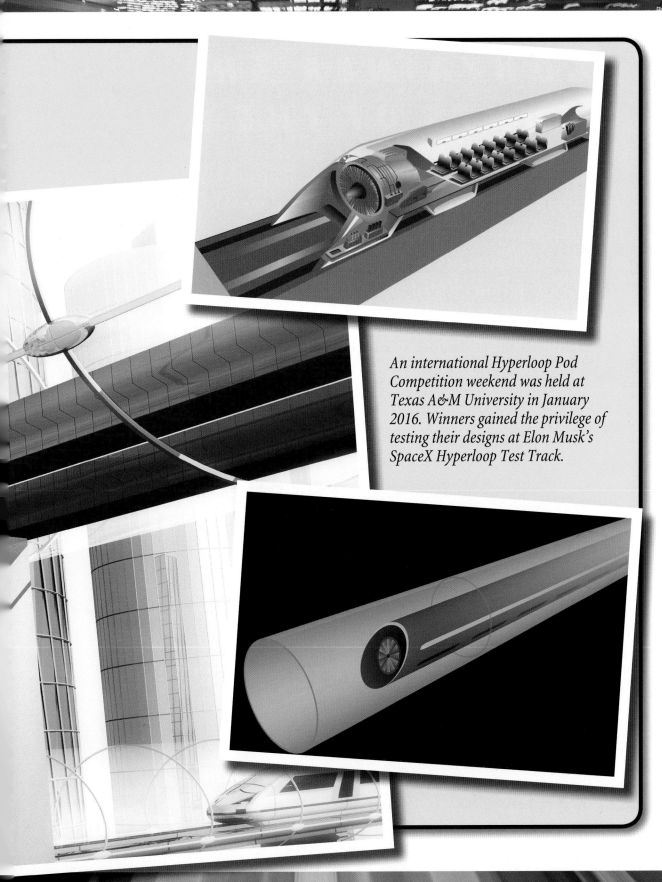

An international Hyperloop Pod Competition weekend was held at Texas A&M University in January 2016. Winners gained the privilege of testing their designs at Elon Musk's SpaceX Hyperloop Test Track.

CONTAINER SHIPS: GIANTS OF THE SEAS

Chances are most everything you're wearing traveled across the ocean on a container ship. One container is large enough to hold 50 or 60 refrigerators, and many container ships carry about 11,000 containers. For that number of containers to be loaded on a train instead of a ship, the train would have to be 44 miles (71 kilometers) long. Yet that huge ship probably had only about 13 people working on it.

How does such a small number of employees keep straight what cargo is in which container and in what order to load and unload the containers? And how does the ship stay balanced and not tip over as it is unloaded? Technology! Advanced computer systems are essential for operating these giants of the seas.

CORNELIA MÆRSK
KALUNDBORG

A container ship will take a shortcut when it can. You've probably taken a shortcut through an alleyway or through a neighbor's backyard. That's just what ships do when they opt to go through the Panama Canal rather than around the tip of South America. In 2007, engineers began a major upgrade on the canal. The upgrade is designed to allow ships carrying about two and a half times as many containers as before to pass through.

STEAM Fast Fact!

The word Panamax is a short way to say Panama Maximum. It describes the size of a ship that is not too large to go through the original Panama Canal. The larger ships that can pass after the upgrade are called Post-Panamax.

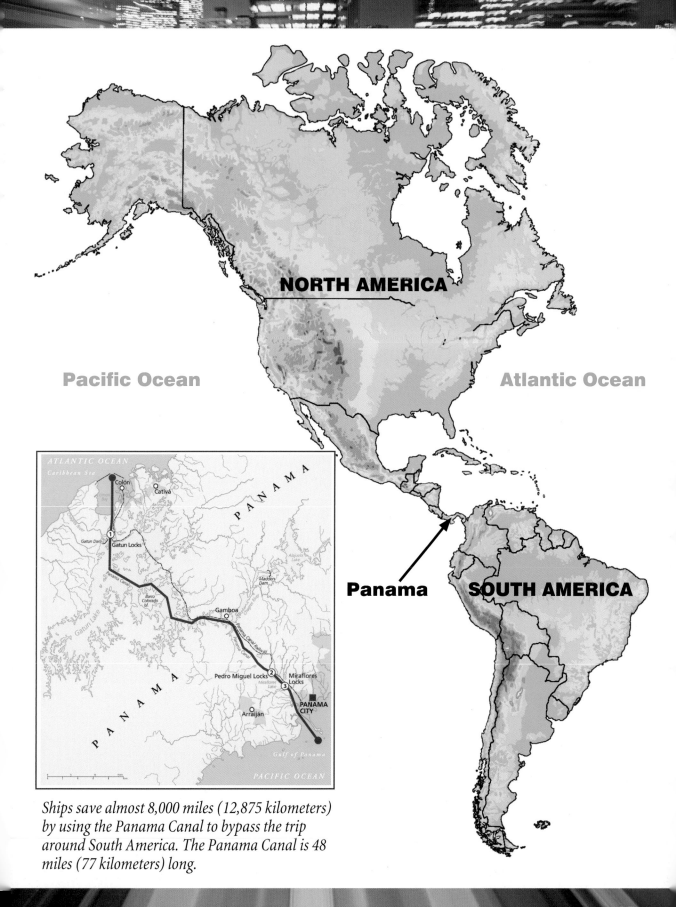

Ships save almost 8,000 miles (12,875 kilometers) by using the Panama Canal to bypass the trip around South America. The Panama Canal is 48 miles (77 kilometers) long.

The president of nearby Nicaragua announced that an even bigger canal would be built in his country, but its future is uncertain. Some scientists are concerned about the effects of that canal on wetlands and rainforests, and about pollution of Lake Nicaragua. The canal route is in a hurricane belt, and a hurricane could cause the canal to flood, threatening lives and property.

Another development in shipping is adding sails to help power ships. Advanced technology makes it possible to collect data about the **efficiency** of different designs. Shippers have tried a few huge sails, numerous smaller sails, and kites that fly high in the sky above the ship to pull it along. One company is even experimenting with a design where the ship's hull, or body, itself acts as a sail!

So far, none of these experiments have convinced shippers that one design works best. Maybe in the future, you will be the clever engineer who makes that discovery!

DRONES: WHAT'S THE BUZZ?

Could an Unmanned Aerial Vehicle (UAV), also known as a drone, be spying on your house? Could one hit you on the head as you walk down the street? Those are not happy thoughts. But consider this: If you become the victim of a flood or tornado, a drone on a search and rescue mission might spot you and save your life. How welcome its buzz would be then!

The remote pilot of a drone must understand the terms used for how it rotates on three axes:

- Roll refers to rotation on the front-to-back axis.
- Pitch refers to rotation on the side-to-side axis.
- Yaw refers to rotation on the vertical axis.

American lawmakers are struggling with how to regulate drones. But one thing is certain: people and organizations are hungry for the data that drones can capture, and for the services they can provide. Although often associated with warfare, drones can also serve **humanitarian** purposes.

STEAM
Fast Fact !

Most drones fly at low **altitudes**, but NASA sent a drone to 62,000 feet (19,000 kilometers), over the eye of Hurricane Edouard in 2014. NASA's drone dropped scientific instruments into the storm to measure temperature, humidity, and winds.

In a developing country, the rainy season can make many roads impassable for part of every year. Disasters, like earthquakes, can make normal delivery methods difficult or impossible in a variety of locations. According to Paola Santana, co-founder of a company called Matternet, even a small delivery of medical supplies can sometimes save a life.

Matternet has operated trial programs in Haiti and Bhutan. A supply of drones is one **component** of its system, which also includes a network of ground stations and the software to control them. Flying between 164 and 328 feet (50 and 100 meters) above ground, Matternet's drones can carry two pounds (.9 kilograms) of cargo more than 12 miles (19 kilometers) on a single battery charge. A parachute would open to slow the descent of a drone in trouble.

In addition to delivering needed supplies, drones are used to map areas damaged by earthquakes, floods, and other disasters.

Another organization, Conservation Drones, helps people use drones in developing countries for a different purpose: to survey wildlife and to monitor, map, and protect ecosystems. Its founders, biologists Lian Pin Koh and Serge Wich, knew that lawbreakers were destroying sections of the rainforest in Indonesia. They feared the destruction would leave the area's orangutans, which nest high in the trees, with too little to eat.

Until 2012, the chances the orangutans would be caught on film resting in their nests or snacking on fruit were as remote as their habitat. But the use of drones for surveying the orangutans has provided a far more effective method than trudging through the jungle. Computer scientists worked with the biologists to automatically count the orangutans captured in thousands of photographs taken by the drones' cameras.

Do you think the overall effect of drones will be to make our world a better place, or a more frightening one?

Aerial photographs taken by drones are used to produce three-dimensional computer models of forests. The photos provide valuable data.

ROCKETS AND ROVERS: WHAT'S UP IN SPACE?

GPS Satellite

You probably seldom think about the manmade or artificial satellites that orbit far above the Earth. But if they vanished, your television screen would likely go black. You wouldn't know whether to pack your umbrella or sunglasses, and you'd unfold a map instead of relying on GPS (Global Positioning System).

SATELLITE COMPARISONS

Type	about the size of...	Altitude	Orbits Earth every...
ISS	football field	230 miles (254 kilometers)	90 minutes
GPS	car	12, 540 miles (20,181 kilometers)	12 hours
Weather & Communication	school bus	22,236 miles (35,785 kilometers)	24 hours

STEAM
Fast Fact !

The International Space Station (ISS), a laboratory with six people onboard, is the largest artificial satellite. It weighs almost one million pounds (453,592 kilograms). NASA will send you a text message to let you know when you can see it.
Sign up at http://spotthestation.nasa.gov.

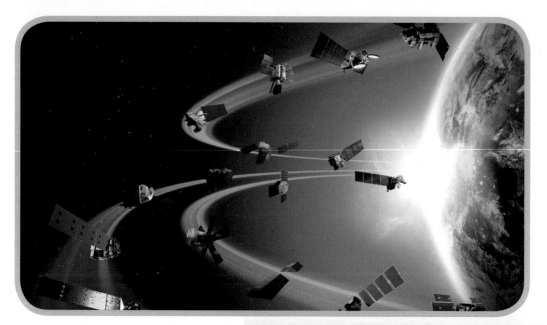

Satellites stay in orbit around the Earth in accordance with Newton's Laws of Motion. They circle at a distance where the centrifugal force pushing them away from Earth equals the force of gravity pulling them back toward the Earth. But first, a rocket has to get them there.

A new American spacecraft called Starliner *will soon take NASA astronauts to the ISS. It will be launched on top of an* Atlas V *rocket.*

STEAM
Fast Fact!

No one rocket had to get the ISS into orbit because it traveled to space one piece or module at a time. NASA is working, though, on a super-powerful rocket called the *Space Launch System* that could transport astronauts to Mars.

Working in agreement with NASA, SpaceX is moving towards its goal of delivering humans into space with the Dragon spacecraft and Falcon 9 rocket.

In 2015, the *Falcon 9* rocket of American company SpaceX celebrated a breakthrough achievement on a mission that put 11 satellites into orbit. The *Falcon 9* has two stages, or sections, that separate from each other at an altitude of about 62 miles (100 kilometers). Its first stage is 14 stories high and has nine engines. At about 37 million dollars, it's by far the most expensive part of the rocket.

After separating from the second stage, the first stage of a rocket typically breaks apart as it falls back to Earth. But the first stage of the *Falcon 9* flipped itself over, relit its engines, and returned to Earth near its launch pad, able to be reused. If reusing rockets becomes routine, the cost of space flight will plummet. It will be like going from needing to buy a new car for every trip, to being able to use the same one time after time.

Making reusable rockets will be a step towards sending people to Mars. NASA has a goal of "putting boot prints on the Red Planet." If humans do land there, how will they get around?

The latest vehicle to explore the surface of Mars is the American rover *Curiosity*, a car-sized, six-wheeled robot. A spacecraft lowered it onto Mars in 2012. Its main purpose is to discover whether Mars is **habitable**. It is also testing the sort of tires and balance controls needed for moving over the rocky terrain.

Do you hope that humans can become a multi-planetary species? Or would you rather keep your feet planted firmly here on Earth?

Curiosity

CARS: WHEN LESS IS MORE

What would you include in a plan for an ideal city? You might want parks for picnics and sports, and plazas where people could sit outside and breathe fresh air. The streets would not be **congested**. Getting to school or work would be stress-free.

The world's population is more and more concentrated in cities, or **urban** areas. City governments are looking for ways to make their cities more habitable. A common strategy is to discourage the use of cars. When cars take up less space, there is more space for people.

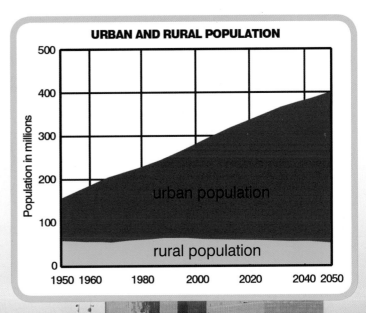

URBAN AND RURAL POPULATION

urban population

rural population

STEAM
Fast Fact!

The city of San Francisco used technology to begin a new parking system in 2011. Spaces with electronic sensors and computerized meters able to change prices reduce the number of drivers circling for a space. Other cities have copied this system.

33

New York City Transportation Commissioner Janette Sadik-Khan wanted to make her city's streets better for active transportation, such as walking and biking. She described her boss, the mayor, as "data-driven." So, she collected data, including counts of cars and people on the streets, to set goals for change. Then she used temporary materials, including paint, barrels, and lawn chairs, for blocking off streets and creating plazas. She collected more data before installing a permanent design.

New York City's historic Union Square Park is a model for other cities reducing the presence of cars.

Bike-friendly practices reduce the presence of cars in New York and other cities. Electronic bicycle barometers record and display the number of bicyclists passing a location. The riders feel good knowing they are part of a growing trend and the cities collect valuable data that shapes policies. For example, bike-sharing services are appearing in more and more cities.

More than 700 cities around the world have bike-share programs.

STEAM
Fast Fact!

Artist Daan Roosegaarde created a bike path in Holland to give riders the feeling of moving through the famous sky from Vincent Van Gogh's painting *Starry Night*. Thousands of lights twinkle like stars. The lights collect solar energy during the day and glow at night.

E-bike use is also on the rise. These bikes use small electric motors, but only when their riders need a little boost. Otherwise, the bikes give their riders the chance to pedal all they want. Engineers have created small batteries for the bikes that are light and hardly noticeable. A 60 mile (97 kilometer) trip might cost as little as ten cents.

E-bikes use batteries that can be recharged at charging stations. Some stations are solar-powered.

Touchscreens at bus stops often show riders how buses connect with trains or subways.

Cities are also taking steps to increase the number of people using buses. Digital screens at some bus stops show the location of buses in real time. Passengers can pay at a kiosk while they wait, making boarding more efficient.

Bus or bike share? Smartphone apps help travelers in a city choose the best option.

Smartphone apps help city dwellers and visitors plan their bus travel. Some cities even have special lanes and traffic signals with sensors that give priority to buses.

Enrique Penalosa, a leader in the South American country of Colombia, has suggested that new cities build many streets where only buses, bicycles, and pedestrians are allowed. Would you enjoy living in a city like that?

NANOTECHNOLOGY: TRANSFORMING TRANSPORTATION

One day, you might hold your bike frame up with one finger. The bridge you ride across might heal its own cracks. You might even travel to space in an elevator. What do these possibilities have in common? Nanotechnology. What exactly is nanotechnology?

See that question mark at the end of this sentence? The dot at its base is about a million nanometers wide, far too big to be nanoscale, which ranges from 1 to 100 nanometers. Everything on Earth is made of tiny particles called atoms and molecules.

Water molecule
10^{-1} nm

Gold atom
3×10^{-1} nm

Glucose molecule
1 nm

Hemoglobin
5 nm

DNA
10 nm

Virus

100 nm

Bacteria
1000 nm

Red cells

10000 nm

Hair
100000 nm

Ant
10^6 nm

A nanometer is one one-billionth of a meter. Nano comes from the Greek word meaning dwarf.

Nanoscience and nanotechnology involve the ability to see and to manipulate those individual particles, with uses in chemistry, physics, biology, materials science, and engineering. Some people are even calling our current time period the Age of Nano.

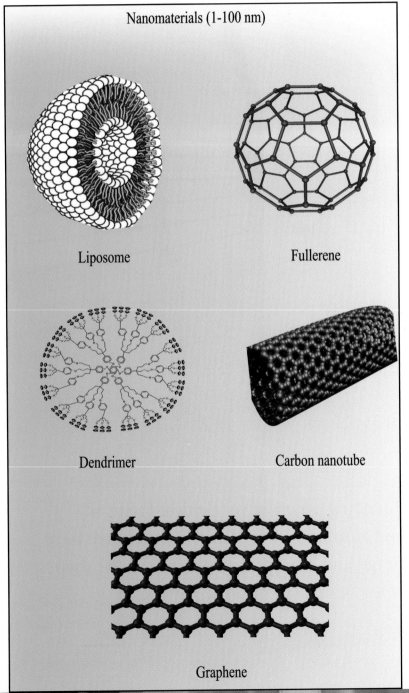

Nanomaterials (1-100 nm)

Liposome

Fullerene

Dendrimer

Carbon nanotube

Graphene

At the nanoscale, even atoms of the same element, such as carbon, differ in their structure. Graphene, fullerene, and carbon nanotubes are all forms of carbon.

Nanotechnology is influencing even the very oldest forms of transportation: walking and running. Many athletic shoes now have soft particles to absorb energy and hard particles to retain the shape. These particles are molecules, which fall into the nanoscale.

Nanocoatings on windshields may one day make windshield wipers obsolete.

Nanotechnology is also increasing the safety and efficiency of the cars we drive. Windshields treated with a nanotech coating remain clear because they **repel** rain, snow, ice, dirt, and bugs.

Nanomaterials in car engines reduce friction to decrease the amount of fuel that is needed. Tires on a toy car have even demonstrated that a nanomaterial can convert the friction from rolling tires into usable energy.

Wires control the operation of cars, ships, aircraft, and spacecraft. New wires created through nanotechnology weigh just a fraction of older ones. Since launching even a single kilogram into space costs about 20,000 U.S. dollars, using lightweight nanomaterials provides a huge savings. Aerogel, a nanomaterial composed of 99.98 percent air, is used to **insulate** the Mars rovers from the frigid Martian climate.

Nanomaterials give car tires a longer life, benefitting the environment.

Tires on Mars have to withstand ground temperatures as low as minus 131.8 degrees Fahrenheit (minus 91 degrees Celsius).

Highways and bridges are benefiting from nanotechnology, as well. Concrete that contains nanomaterials is less likely to **corrode**. Reflective paint containing nanoscale glass creates road markings that are highly visible and durable. Nanosensors embedded in bridges and tunnels can detect both mechanical stresses and chemicals that contribute to corrosion.

The super-insulating properties of silica aerogel protect a flower from the blue flame shown below, which is about 2,700 degrees Fahrenheit (1,500° Celsius).

And what about that space elevator? An extremely strong and light nanomaterial may make it possible one day to stretch a cable between Earth and a satellite in space. People and cargo could then achieve Earth orbit without a rocket. Would you press the button for a ride up to the 9,680,000th floor?

STEAM Fast Fact!

Do some scientists think a space elevator is impossible? Of course! No one can see into the future. Lord Kelvin, a prominent scientist, wrote in 1896 that he had not the smallest molecule of faith in aerial navigation other than ballooning. The Wright Brothers' historic flight came seven years later. What marvels of transportation we may see in the years to come!

Transportation relies on professionals in each of the STEAM fields. Science, technology, engineering, art, and math join forces to drive innovation—moving people and goods around the world, and beyond!

Want to Be a Part of Transforming Transportation?

- Attend a meeting of people in your local government who work on transportation issues.
- Participate in a transportation-related event at a science museum or university.
- Visit the Career Corner of the NASA website to learn more about a variety of careers.
- Try taking apart and putting back together a discarded bicycle.
- Be on the lookout for transportation in the news.

Transporting people and cargo to space could cost much less if a nanomaterial was developed to make a space elevator.

GLOSSARY

altitudes (AL-ti-toods): the heights of something above ground or above sea level

component (kuhm-POH-nuhnt): a part of a larger whole, especially a machine or a system

congested (kuhn-JES-tid): so blocked up or full that it is impossible to move

corrode (kuh-RODE): to destroy or eat away at something little by little

efficiency (i-FISH-uhn-see): the quality of working or operating well, quickly, and without waste

entrepreneur (ahn-truh-pruh-NUR): someone who starts businesses and finds new ways to make money

friction (FRIK-shuhn): the force that slows down objects when they rub against each other

habitable (HAB-I-tuh-buhl): safe and good enough for people to live in

humanitarian (hyoo-man-i-TER-ee-uhn): of or having to do with helping people and improving their lives

insulate (IN-suh-late): to cover something with material in order to stop heat, electricity, or sound from escaping

repel (ri-PEL): to drive back or keep away

urban (UR-buhn): having to do with or living in a city

INDEX

SHOW WHAT YOU KNOW

1. What are the advantages and disadvantages of crowdsourcing?
2. Brainstorm some situations where a drone would be a better choice than a person for making deliveries.
3. How do manmade satellites change our lives?
4. Why are the efforts to make rockets reusable important?
5. What are some ways that nanotechnology is changing transportation?

WEBSITES TO VISIT

www.nano.gov/education-training/k12

www.nasa.gov/audience/forstudents

www.howthingsfly.si.edu

About The Author

Ruth M. Kirk writes nonfiction for young readers from her home in North Carolina, and also teaches English as a Second Language. She would take most any form of transportation to visit the special people in her life.

Meet The Author!
www.meetREMauthors.com

www.rourkeeducationalmedia.com

PHOTO CREDITS: Cover: fast motion background © Melpomene, drone© Chaikom; page 4-5 bus © legend, cargo ship © LovePHY, rocket © 3Dsculptor; page 6 Hyperloop art © Camilo Sanchez, page 6 © chombosan, page 7 air hockey table © Sergey Ryzhov, bicycle brake © supot phanna, speed skater © Dmitry Yashkin, parachutist © Nikishkin Andrey, Earthquake slabs diagram © Designua, aerial view of fault © Ikluft, Elon Musk photo © Steve Jurvetson; pages 10-11 large illustration © andrey_l, small illustration top © Camilo Sanchez https://creativecommons.org/licenses/by-sa/4.0/deed.en , small illustration bottom © chombosan; page 12-13 © VladSV, page 13 © Chalalai Atcha; page 14-15 photo ships © BlackMac, map of canal © Peter Hermes Furian, map of North and South America © Bardocz Peter; page 16 map of Nicaragua © Rainer Lesniewski, page 17 © Reederei Wessels/Fotoflite; page 18-19 drone © Alexey Yuzhakov, drone in crowd © ChameleonsEye, page 18 small photo © Stock image; page 20 drone © gualtiero buffi, page 21 earthquake town © arindambanerjee, page 20-21 earthquake rural © Everything; page 22-23 © guentermanaus, page 23 © Kate Capture; page 24-25 satellite © Andrey Armyagov, ISS courtesy of NASA, football field © phoenix; page 26 courtesy NASA/JPL-Caltech, , page 27 and 28-29 courtesy of NASA; page 29 courtesy NASA/Amber Watson; page 30-31 © NASA/JPL-Caltech/MSSS and NASA, ESA, and The Hubble Heritage Team (STScI/AURA); Page 32-33 central park © SurangaSL, page 33 San Fransisco © archana bhartia; page 34-35 © Sean Pavone, page 35 © pisaphotography, Daan Roosegaarde; page 36 © JFs Pic Factory, page 37 © GaudiLab, Georgejmclittle, page 38-39 © Sureshbup Wikipedia source: http://www.mdpi.com/1422-0067/15/5/7158; page 40-41 © lzf, page 41 windshields © Valerio Pardi; page 42 car in snow © Nneirda, pages 42-44 courtesy of NASA/JPL, page 44-45 diagram © Skyway at en.wikipedia / User:Booyabazooka. All images from Shutterstock.com except: San Andreas fault page 8, Elon Musk page 9, images pages 17, 26-31, 35 (bottom photo), pages 42 (Mars rover) and page 43 and 45

Edited by: Keli Sipperley

Cover and Interior design by: Nicola Stratford   www.nicolastratford.com

Library of Congress PCN Data

STEAM Guides in Transportation / Ruth M. Kirk
(STEAM Every Day)
ISBN 978-1-68191-707-8 (hard cover)
ISBN 978-1-68191-808-2 (soft cover)
ISBN 978-1-68191-904-1 (e-Book)

Library of Congress Control Number: 2016932585

Rourke Educational Media
Printed in the United States of America, North Mankato, Minnesota

Also Available as:

ROURKE'S
e-Books